PAYING FOR THE DREAM

How to Thrive on Your Homestead

Book 3 in the Get Out of the City and Thrive Series

By Robyn Dolan

Robyn Dolan

Paying for the Dream

How to Thrive on Your Homestead

Book 3 in the Get Out of the City and Thrive Series

Disclaimer

Thank you for purchasing "Paying for the Dream – How to Thrive on Your Homestead" Book 3 in the Get Out of the City and Thrive Series. I hope you find it enjoyable, entertaining and helpful.

All persons in this book are real, though most of the names have been changed to protect the innocent (me). Some persons are composites of several different individuals, no likeness to one particular person is intended and composites are used merely for the author's convenience in illustrating a point. All information presented in this work is considered correct as of the time of its writing. All information is presented for educational and entertainment purposes only, no warranties are made and author assumes no responsibility or liability for misuse or misunderstanding of this information or damages due to use of information contained in this book.

This book details the author's personal experiences with and opinions about moving out of the city and making major life changes. The author is not licensed or certified to teach or give legal or medical advice. This book is not a substitute for legal, medical or accounting advice from a licensed professional.

This book provides content related to relocation, lifestyle and employment changes and homesteading topics. As such, use of this book implies your acceptance of this disclaimer.

To my dad, Bob Siemann. You were the answer to a little girl's prayers, my biggest cheerleader, and my safe harbor. I love you always.

Acknowledgements

So many people help to write a book. First and foremost, thanks be to God, for the inspiration and constant unrest until I am doing what (I hope) He seems to want. To Yak, for putting up with mom's writing moods and learning curves. To Maryruth and Charles, who never let up in encouraging me to write and plow into the book business. To my older children, for not putting me in the psych ward. Yet. To Jonah and Aiden, for keeping me young. To Richard and Angela Hoy and Writersweekly.com, and all my other online mentors for educating me. To my parents, for not being overly disappointed that I did not choose law or medicine as my vocation. To the folks at Grit Magazine, for letting me in as one of their reader bloggers back in 2008, and occasionally using my work in their publications.

CONTENTS

INTRODUCTION

Many people dream, at one time or another, of leaving the city and enjoying a "simpler" life in the country. Many of these never pursue that dream. If it is because of fear, set that aside. It is very doable. The process and timing are not the same for everyone who attempts to move to the country. However, the basics are.

I outlined how I did it in Book 1 of this series: Get Out of the City and Thrive – How I did it and How You Can, Too!, which is available on Amazon. In a nutshell: get the family on board, make a financial plan, start making the adjustments to your lifestyle and set a date. Investigate the areas you are interested in, ways to make a living in those areas and whether you can achieve the lifestyle you are aiming for there.

Book 2: Milking the Wild Goat - How to Find Land and Set up Your Homestead, is also available on Amazon. In it, I go into detail about land, housing, garden, critters, and more.

If you are reading this book, I am assuming you have read Book 1: Get Out of the City and Thrive – How I did it and How You Can, Too! and Book 2: Milking the Wild Goat - How to Find Land and Set up Your Homestead and really want to decide if you can make a go of it as a homesteader. The final ingredient is income. So how will you pay for the dream and thrive?

It seems that today, only the "lucky" ones have "traditional" jobs. With steady hours, reliable paychecks, health insurance, paid vacations, and pensions. Most of the rest of us have "income streams".

HOW AM I GOING TO PAY FOR ALL OF THIS?

When I first moved to Arizona, I had a bit of savings to get us by for a few months while I built up my home business. The trouble was, my children were pre- and early teens and still needed supervision. In addition, we were homeschooling. My business required that I get products in front of people and be able to promote them like a grown-up. Not like a harried mom trying to get children to do their schoolwork, behave, and run a business all at once. So before the money ran out, I got a job. As a bartender at a local dinner house. A steady progression of better jobs finally led to me becoming self-employed once again. I cleaned houses and brought my youngest son with me. I made soaps and sold them at craft fairs. I learned how to build a website and opened an on-line store. Then I built another website and opened a couple more online stores. I started blogging, free-lance writing, and writing books. Doing farmers markets and bigger craft shows. I sold milk from my cow and goats; eggs from my chickens; beef from my beef steers. This was my way of making ends meet. There are many more, depending on your talents, abilities, and requirements.

It seems that today, only the "lucky" ones have "traditional" jobs. With steady hours, reliable pay-checks, health insurance, paid vacations, and pensions. Most of the rest of us have "income streams". So do not panic if you cannot find the coveted 9-5. It has become quite common to piece together a living a little here, a little there. Think "outside the box", as they say. Maybe you will have a part-time job with a paycheck, a side business, and sell some of your homestead products. Outside the big city, this is becoming the new normal. (Even in the big city.)

Before you jump into job hunting, take your work history into consideration. Check out the job market. Research the need and market for your services. Look at the competition. Think about what you have always wanted to do and what your talents and abilities are. What kind of lifestyle do you want to achieve? Do you want to work from home? Be out around people? Set your own schedule? Just get a paycheck? Think about all these things and then see what is available. Always start out with a plan. And a back up. And a back-up-back-up. None of them may work out, but eventually something will.

> *Review your resume. Don't worry, you are the only one who is going to see this. So go ahead and include that job in the dive bar and that retail management job where you were fired for telling your team that they needed to do their jobs.*

WORK HISTORY

R eview your resume. Don't worry, you are the only one who is going to see this. So go ahead and include that job in the dive bar and that retail management job where you were fired for telling your team that they needed to do their jobs. Include that lawn mowing business you started when you were 10. And that warehouse job where you told the manager exactly what you thought of him. And got fired.

Which jobs did you love?

Think about why you loved those jobs. Try to pick out the qualities that made it worth going into work every day. Make a list of those qualities and try to aim for a job that has them.

Hate?

Again, why did you hate that job? Pick out the problems and try to avoid jobs that have those same problems.

Tolerate for the paycheck?

What exactly was it about this job that made you able to suit up and show up every day so that you could get paid? Or was it more the circumstances in your life at the time?

What, exactly, made the difference in how you felt about each job?

Was it your boss(es), coworkers, the work itself, the customers?

Which jobs are you physically no longer (or soon to be no longer) able to do?

Some jobs require physical labor. Restaurant and bar workers typically need to be able to lift and balance heavy trays, laden with food and drink. House cleaners need to be able to bend and scrub, lift and move moderately heavy objects. Construction workers need to be able to handle power tools, lift, and move heavy materials. Truck drivers need to be able to sit for long periods of time.

Which jobs have been easy to get?

There has always been and will always be a demand for skilled labor. Same for house cleaners, gardeners, carpenters, repair people, etc. Nevertheless, do not let that make you complacent. That does not guarantee you work. If you are moving to a rural area, hoping to live for less money, chances are very good that most of your neighbors will have the same idea. They probably will not be looking for house cleaners, gardeners or repair people. If you are near a larger town, though, with a resort, or a population that has higher paying jobs, you might have a market. Check it out. Use the next few chapters as a guideline.

Check out the job market in the area you are considering moving to. Pick up a local paper, or several.

JOB MARKET

Check out the job market in the area you are considering moving to.

Pick up a local paper, or several. Look through the want ads. Check Craig's list for your prospective area. Try other job boards for the area you want to move to. Some websites currently posting employment opportunities include:

Coolworks.com
Careerbuilder.com
Monster.com
USA Jobs
indeed.com
simplyhired.com

What jobs are available?

See if there is anything that interests you. Look for jobs you have done before, that you might be well qualified for. Decide if there are enough possibilities to make it worth looking for work. Maybe even put your resume out there.

What are the requirements?

If there are too many applicants, companies narrow the field by requiring certain minimum qualifications. College degrees, prior experience, certifications, specialized training are all ways to narrow the field of applicants. Conversely, if there are too few applicants, companies will sometimes relax their requirements, depending on the position. Do not let requirements hold you back from applying.

What is the pay? Is it enough?

Sure, you can always fall back on slinging burgers. However, can you realistically live on that, even if you radically minimize? Something better does not always come along. Sometimes it takes quite a while before it does. You should have a clear idea of how much money you need each month. If the job does not satisfy, keep looking, or consider looking in another location.

Are these options suitable for permanent employment, or just to get by while you get your business established?

See above. However, if you are planning to get your own business up and running, you may be able to get by with just a "ramen noodle" paycheck. Use the guidelines in the next couple of chapters to help you do some extensive research on the prospects for the success of your business, first.

If you are setting up a business, do the available options pay enough to keep you going and give you enough time to work your side hustle?

Time. If you have to work 60 hours a week at your "job", you are not going to have much time to get your side hustle going. If you can squeeze by part-time and still survive while you get your "real" business established, you will get it done a lot faster and be a much happier camper.

Age, family size, income, occupation, employment, industry, and housing will certainly affect what kind of products/services will sell in the area you are considering, or if you will need to go out of the area to sell.

SELF EMPLOYMENT

– research the need and market for your product/services

W hat are the demographics of the area you are considering moving to?

Age, family size, income, occupation, employment, industry, housing?

This will certainly affect what kind of products/services will sell in that area, or if you will need to go out of the area to sell.

To research demographics, type the city and state into the address bar of your internet home page and click search. Frequently, Wikipedia will be one of the first entries. It will provide basic info, including geography, history, and demographics. Wikipedia is user generated, meaning anyone can post and edit entries, so do not rely upon it as your final source of information. It will also usually provide references and links to further info.

City-Data brings up quite a bit of information to add to your research, using government and private sources. Can include crime and weather stats, too. Type in your city and state. http://www.city-data.com

Suburban Stats provides population stats by age, gender and race. Enter your city and state in the search bar. https://suburbanstats.org/population/

United States Census Bureau has tools to research population, geography, economy and more. Type your parameters into the search bar. https://www.census.gov/en.html

Zip Lookup has you enter your zip code to get info

on area lifestyle, income, age, and population density. http://www.esri.com/data/esri_data/ziptapestry

The Small Business Administration offers tons of tools and information for starting your small business. Including market research tools. https://www.sba.gov/starting-business/how-start-business/business-data-statistics/demographics

What product or service are you planning to provide?

You can research several ideas and decide which one might be the most viable for the area you are considering. Having a variety of useful skills gives you more options for relocating and starting your own business. More so if they don't require licensing in that particular area. Check each location to see if your particular product or service requires a license or certification. For instance, nursing care always does. Elder companionship, household help, assistance with daily activities such as bathing, meal preparation, and toileting may or may not.

How much will you charge?

Consider whether you will charge by the hour or by the job. This depends, again, on your product or service. If you are selling products, you need to factor in materials, labor, shipping, and utilities or cost of delivering the product to the customer. Do not short yourself on labor. Your time is valuable. See what others in the area are charging. If you don't think you can survive on that amount, rethink your product or service.

How much profit do you need to pay your bills, taxes, etc.?

If you don't have a budget now, it's time to make one. You need to be able to estimate your cost of living in order to make wise decisions about pricing, job bids, and hourly wages. Add up every bill you have for the year, divide by 12 and that is your average monthly expense. Pad it a little for emergencies and unexpected expenses. Now you know about what you need to make per month. Divide that by how many hours you want to work. Then figure out how many hours/jobs you need to work to make your living. Is this realistic? If not, rethink your plan.

How many customers do you need to reach your minimum profit level?

If you are charging by the job, how many jobs will

you need each day or week? Figure out how many hours it takes to complete each job and then figure out how many jobs you are able to complete each week. Will you need to hire employees in order to complete enough jobs? Then, of course, your expenses go up, with having to pay employees or subcontractors and that is a whole 'nuther can of worms for another book.

If you are making products, what is your average sale? How many sales would you need to make each day or week? How many people do you need to pitch before you get a buyer? How far afield would you have to go to reach that many potential customers? That will create more expense.

If you are charging hourly, keep in mind that there are only so many hours in a day and you don't want to be spending all of them working. You will have to be very careful about charging enough to live on, as well as keep reasonable hours.

How many other businesses are providing similar products or services?

If the market is already saturated, you may want to rethink your business idea or check out a different location.

If you are looking at a small town, do not rely

on an internet search to provide this information. You will really need to visit the location in person, pick up a few local papers – newspaper, newsletter, local free classifieds paper, etc. Look through them. Check bulletin boards in local businesses – gas stations, markets, supermarkets, convenience stores, feed stores, post office, etc. Many small businesses in rural areas do not list themselves or advertise on the internet. They rely on word of mouth and local free advertising.

Once you get serious about a location, if your other research indicates that this is a good prospect, it is a wise idea to spend several days at a time in the area, during different parts of the year, to get a feel for whether your conclusions from your other research are accurate.

If the population of the area you are consider-ing is 100, and they are all retirees living on small, fixed incomes, how much business do you think your $20/hr repair person service is going to get, even if $20/hr is a screamin' deal for repair person service?

EVALUATE THE COMPETITION

Look at other businesses in the area. Demographics will also give you an idea of who is competing for jobs. Are there dozens of repair person services, plumbers, secretarial or tax services advertised? How will you stand out? On the other hand, maybe there is a need for commercial cleaning services (offices or hotels, etc.) which is underprovided. Discover if there is a gap your service can fill.

If the population of the area you are considering is 100, and they are all retirees living on small, fixed incomes, how much business do you think your $50/hr repair person service is going to get, even if $50/hr is a screamin' deal for repair person service?

If the population of the surrounding areas is a few thousand, and the demographics include a large number of professional households, then maybe $50/hr is too low to charge. Then, again, if there are 100 repair person services in the same area, you might have a hard time getting anyone even to notice you.

Next, look at businesses that offer the same types of services you are planning to offer. For bigger cities, you can search online. Since this book is about getting out of the city, we will assume that you are relocating to a more rural area. Many of the businesses competing with yours will not be listed online. Nevertheless, search there first, anyway. Now pick up local newspapers and other circulars such as the local version of Dollar Saver, Buffalo Nickel, Coffee Talk, or other free classified advertising publication. Sometimes just a cursory glance will tell you that there are already two dozen repair person or house cleaner services in the area. If not, delve deeper. Go to local stores, the library, and the post office, and check their bulletin boards. Many small operators just post a flyer with their service and phone number listed.

If it looks like there might still be a demand for your type of business, call a few of the existing businesses and see what they are charging. Compare that to the rate you plan to charge. Is your rate too high? Too low? Will you be able to charge enough to make a living?

Read on for more tips on starting your own business. I have included more resources at the end of the book.

> *Use your imagination to try to morph your present reality, stage by stage, into your future ideal. This is just dream time but you may come up with some insights into what you can do to make headway into your new life.*

WHAT IS YOUR IDEAL JOB

Really envision yourself living the life you dream of. Doing work that you love. Now take stock of where you're at and how far off that dream is. Use your imagination to try to morph your present reality, stage by stage, into your future ideal. This is just dream time but you may come up with some insights into what you can do to make headway into your new life. Write your ideas down in a notebook that you can come back to and revise and add to as you journey down this path of major life change.

Back to reality.

Of course, we could all find a way to scrape by with a passive income of $10,000 per month, couldn't we?

However "realistically", what hours, pay, type of work, do you think would be the ideal situation for you? Does that seem to exist? Adjust your dream expectations and try to get them closer to reality.

Base this investigation on your work history. Remember, you are looking at your entire, including "secret" work history. Think about whether or not you plan to start a side hustle (which will require a few hours of its own). Decide what hours you prefer to work, the minimum wage you need to make, and how far you are willing to commute. This will help you to decide what job options you will consider.

Are you seeing your ideal situation on the job boards, in the local papers, or on bulletin boards? If so, put out some feelers. Maybe even a few applications or resumes. Far better to go in with a job than not.

If you are not seeing this situation, examine what is available, and decide what compromises you are willing to make.

Here, you want to think about skills you have that you may not have used in your previous employment. You may discover a latent ability that will open up new options for you in business, homesteading, or employment.

WHAT ARE YOUR TALENTS AND ABILITIES

Here, you want to think about skills you have that you may not have used in your previous employment. You may discover a latent ability that will open up new options for you in business, homesteading, or employment.

Are you good at managing people?

How frustrated do you get when people don't do what you want? Do you feel like firing them, or do you look for ways to get them to invest themselves in the work?

Good managers are also always in demand, but walking into a management position is not always easy. You may have to start out at a lower level and work your way up.

Delegation?

Are you someone who can turn over a task to another and let it go? Or do you need to control every situation and end up doing everything yourself so it gets done "right"? Do you feel confident in your ability to communicate clearly and have your expectations met?

Sales?

Do you have the stomach to eat rejection for breakfast, lunch, and dinner? Sales is a numbers game. Those numbers are high. Learn how to sort through the less likely prospects and concentrate on following up with the ones who are more likely to buy now.

Salespeople are always in demand. Sales positions, however, do not usually come with a living wage, if they have any kind of wage attached. Commission is normally how salespeople are paid, and payment arrives only when the deal is closed.

Are you good at mechanics, carpentry, and heavy equipment?

Many rural areas have mining, construction, farming, or other labor industries. A good mechanic is always in demand, but you might have to open your own shop.

Are you a gentle caregiver?

If the average age of your local population is over 60, it is likely that there will be a market for caregiver/companion services. This can involve anything from just providing companionship to an older person, while their younger family member is away at work or for a break, to full on nursing home care. While providing skilled medical care requires certain licenses and certifications, cooking, clean-ing, and generally assisting with activities of daily living, does not. Providing care to an elderly person can be a challenge, however. Especially if that per-son has Alzheimer's or dementia.

Providing day care for children does require some licensing and certification. The hazards inherent on a homestead, as well as the more remote location of the typical homestead make this a bad idea if you are out in the boonies. If, however, you are in town, this might be a consideration. A small, fenced yard, where children can play safely, and a highly visible, easily accessible location make drop-off and pick-up more convenient, and help to discourage any un-founded accusations.

Efficient cook and cleaner?

Cook up some extra meals, package, and freeze them. Figure out your cost and add a few dollars. Offer them to elderly, homebound, and disabled people. Check with your local health department to see if permits are required. List ingredients meticulously, as well as reheating instructions.

Figure out an hourly rate for basic home cleaning – vacuum/mop, dust, and sanitize. Figure out rates for deep clean, organizing, window washing, etc., if you want to offer that. Remember that home sizes and styles vary greatly. Use your hourly rate for a basis, but inspect the job before you commit to a price.

Do you love working in the yard?

Offer lawn mowing and/or landscaping services. Many rural areas require homeowners to clear a perimeter around their homes during fire season, often referred to as weed abatement. This is another service you can provide. Trees often need trimming away from power lines, even in the country. An ice-laden branch can put excessive weight on a power line, causing it to fall and disconnect power to the house. Live power lines that are down also create a very dangerous situation.

Talking to people

Customer service is important to any business.

Many businesses need receptionists, people to help customers at the counter or in the store, people to help customers troubleshoot problems in person or on the phone, and always an ability to handle customers in a cheerful, positive manner.

WHAT KIND OF LIFESTYLE DO YOU WANT TO ACHIEVE?

Do you want to work from home?

Check out remote opportunities on job boards. If you have a specialty, such as accounting, virtual assistant, writing, web design, contact local businesses and residents to introduce yourself, explain your services, and explore their needs. You might want to set up a website for your business.

Be out around people?

Scout out the local businesses and see which ones might be hiring, or interesting to work at. Who are the customers? Tourists? Locals? Other businesses?

Set your own schedule?

If you have certain hours you are available, like 9-2, while the kids are in school, visit businesses that are only open during those hours and see if they are hiring. If your available hours vary, but you know your schedule in advance, ask about an arrangement where you can give them your available hours a week or two ahead of them making the schedule. If your hours are all over the place, you may be better off working from home.

Just get a paycheck?

Start filling out applications. If your primary goal is just to get a paycheck, you do not have to be too choosy about what the job is. As long as it is legal and within your moral parameters, go for it. If you are hired, you can still continue looking until you find something that is a good fit for the long term.

Sometimes it is worth just walking in off the street and asking if a place is hiring or ask to fill out an application. A job opening might have just occurred, and it saves the manager time and money to fill it immediately.

Ask around. You never know who might have inside info on jobs that just opened up. Sometimes a good word from a current employee is the decisive factor in getting the job.

Robyn Dolan

*The internet has opened up all kinds of possi-
bilities for making a living.*

SOME IDEAS TO CONSIDER

The internet has opened up all kinds of possibilities for making a living. More and more people are becoming location independent and "digital nomads". Not all location independent income opportunities are dependent upon and internet connection, however.

The following chapters outline some ideas for making a living in the more rural and remote areas followed by ways to make money from your homestead produce and projects.

If you plan to work online you will need fast, reliable internet, something not always readily available in rural areas.

ONLINE

I f you plan to work online you will need fast, reliable internet, something not always readily available in rural areas. Satellite internet is very expensive, especially if you need unlimited data. You may also want to do some market research to determine if your particular idea is financially viable. Of course, if you already have an established online business, you are set.

Some easy ways to sell online are:

Etsy – set up an online shop to sell handmade, vintage, or digital products

EBay – online garage sale. Set up as an auction or buy now item. EBay offers many new and refurbished items, especially electronics.

Amazon – set up an online store to sell your used books or anything else. Warehouse your items with

Amazon for a monthly fee.

Register with job boards to find work online. Upwork is one freelance job board. Offer your services and look for jobs to bid on. Other job boards include Fiverr, Indeed, Guru, Monster, and more.

Website – you can set up a website with an online store free, or you can pay a small fee for a domain name and hosting. Offer your services, post samples of your work, offer digital products. Hosting sites include Lowest Hosting, GoDaddy, Blue Host, and many others. Site building tools include Wordpress, Blogger, Squarespace, and GoDaddy.

Teach English – Skype, Google Hangouts or any other online video calling program can enable you to offer private lessons, or even classroom/group lessons. Some brick and mortar schools also hire online teachers. Udemy, Coursera, iTalki, Berlitz, and VIPKid are just a few online schools with teaching opportunities.

Tutor – same as above. Alternatively, you could tutor by email in some subjects. Sites like tutor.com enable you to offer your services, and/or you could offer them on your website. You can also make videos of your subject and sell your services on DVD or as a subscription. YouTube, Vimeo, and other video sites are good places to put up sample lessons with a link to your store.

Teach music – same as above two. Video calls are

best for interaction. Put a couple of lessons up on YouTube or Vimeo. LessonFace, Takelessons, teach-musiconline, and teachable all offer music lessons.

In any online business, be careful about scams. Learn how to protect yourself from false buyers, sellers and others who will steal your products/ financial info.

52

Set yourself up as a consultant and approach local businesses or reach out through the internet to offer your services.

CONSULTING

What are you an expert in? Set yourself up as a consultant and approach local businesses or reach out through the internet to offer your services.

Here are some ideas of professional experts who can offer consulting services:

Legal
Accounting
Taxes
Web design
Retail management
Online marketing
Advertising
Marketing
Engineering
Sales

Consulting can range from expert advice, to actual work on a project, so learn about what others in your field of expertise are offering and charging and start from there. In some cases it might be to your advantage to have a Bachelor's or higher degree in your field of expertise. But not always. Several years of experience in your field can also lend a high degree of credibility to you as a consultant.

Never perform online work with a promise of "check's in the mail". If they are online, they can use Paypal to send a check.

COLLECTING PAYMENT FOR ONLINE SALES/ SERVICES

You can certainly set up payment processing through your bank or other financial institution, but the fees and charges are usually prohibitive for a small business. There are far better options now, such as Paypal, Square, Etsy, ProPay, and many others. Some online conglomerates, such as EBay, Amazon, Etsy, Upwork, Guru (and some other job boards) will collect for you and deal with non-payers and scammers. You will pay them a fee from your earnings, but you will know about that before hand.

Never perform online work with a promise of

"check's in the mail". If they are online, they can use Paypal to send a check.

If you are not comfortable with the client, do not work for them at any price.

OTHER SKILLS

Do your homework before you rely solely on this idea. Have something to fall back on.

Repair person – make up some business cards or a flyer with tear-off tabs to post on bulletin boards at local businesses (with their permission). Hand them out to people you meet. And everywhere.

Uber/Lyft – sign up and pick up/drop off customers where you are available. The company collects the fare, takes a fee for dealing with processing and collecting, and pays you. Customer should still tip.

Grocery shopping service – take care with this. Some customers will try to get this service and their groceries for nothing. Collect payment for groceries in advance, collect your fee and any shortage immediately on delivery. Or do not deliver the goods. Make sure they understand what is non-refundable. Many grocery stores now offer delivery and Instacart is available in many areas. These services take care of the financials for you.

Elder care companion – services can vary from just keeping company, watching a movie, playing a board game, to full on cooking, cleaning, bathing, assisting with dressing, feeding, etc.

House cleaning – a basic house cleaning consists of vacuuming, dusting, and sanitizing bathrooms and kitchen. You should charge extra (negotiated in advance) for washing dishes, laundry, changing sheets, deep cleaning, windows, etc.

House check service for vacationing or absentee owners – this is basically a security check for peace of mind. You go in, look in all the rooms, make sure the water, electric, and other systems are functioning properly, flush the toilets, run each faucet for a moment, etc. Look and listen for leaks, strange noises, evidence of insect or rodent infestation, stains (from leakage or other). Be visible so anyone driving by will assume that someone is home. Do this on a weekly or biweekly basis, at least. Even homeowners using Airbnb or another rental service need someone on the ground to handle keys and troubleshooting.

Construction professionals - carpenters, electricians, plumbers. – check licensing requirements. In California, jobs under $600 do not typically require a licensed professional. A repair person could do them. Projects over $600 usually require a license (in CA). Take out an ad in local papers. Pass out business cards, hang flyers. Word of mouth.

Secretaries, real estate assistants. – visit local businesses and see if they have a need for secretarial, receptionist, or personal assistant services. In some cases, you could freelance for several businesses. Others may want you to keep regular office hours. In a real estate (or other) office you could possibly offer these services to several agents at once.

Pet grooming; mobile services. – you can do this from a stable location or out of your own vehicle. Or you could bring your supplies into the client's location. But then you will have to clean up your mess at every stop.

Always cover yourself when you are going to be alone with someone's elder, child, or pet/home. It is too easy for someone to accuse you of abuse, theft, or neglect. If you are not comfortable with the client, do not work for them at any price.

Do not give the customer a price based on hours only and then add in the labor and materials later and vice versa.

COLLECTING PAYMENT FOR OFFLINE SERVICES

If you are working as an independent contractor for a service like Uber or Lyft, they will collect payment and disburse your portion to you. You may need to request your tip in an unobtrusive manner, if that is not included.

If you are running the whole show, here are some guidelines to start with. You can add, delete, and tweak them to work for you.

Establish your rates.

Decide how you are going to base your charges for

service. Are you going to charge by the hour or by the job?

Give the customer the bottom line up front.

If you break down your pricing by hours, labor, and materials, include all this in your estimate. Do not give the customer a price based on hours only and then add in the labor and materials later and vice versa. You will not get a repeat customer. Moreover, you may not be paid, either. Especially if the customer is paying cash and only has so much. In addition, bounced check fees will further deplete your funds.

Cash is always good.

However not everyone can pay cash or likes to keep a lot of cash lying around. Offering a cash discount will certainly encourage that form of payment.

Accept credit/debit cards.

Nowadays, if you have a smart phone, you can get a card reader that will quickly and securely authorize and charge your customer and get you paid. If you cannot get one through Paypal, try Square, Propay, or one of the many other established services available.

Accepting checks.

Whenever I accept a check, I frankly ask the customer if it is good now, or if I need to hold it. I tell them I will be depositing it with my smartphone immediately, and if that is a problem, I do not accept a check. I offer to deliver the goods when they have the money. Because I have an Etsy shop I can also accept credit cards through the Etsy app on my smartphone.

Salespeople are always in demand.

SALES

Salespeople are always in demand. Keep in mind that most companies will only pay commission, no base salary. So be prepared to tough it out until you close your first sale, which can take months, depending upon your experience and the demand for your product.

Some sales professions include:

Real estate – most states now require that you complete certain classes before you can take the licensing test. Some offices offer training for new agents. Very few offer a weekly paycheck. Sometimes you can start out on a team that has an arrangement to split the commission, or as an assistant to a busy agent, who makes some kind of payment arrangement with you. Once you are ready to go completely on your own, be very careful to adhere to office ethics about stealing clients.

Auto – new and used car dealers can always use a good salesperson. Some offer hourly compensation.

Financial – check with banks, mortgage brokers, etc. some education and training is required. Licensing may be required at some levels.

Insurance – once, again, this usually requires licensing, but most insurance companies take care of the educational requirements and training in-house. This is usually a commission only position.

Direct sales – Avon, Tupperware, Origami Owl (jewelry), Pampered Chef, DoTerra, etc. Most companies offer a starter kit, usually under $100. Most of these companies are some form of multi-level marketing; your senior sales rep gets a percentage of your sales, so it is in their interest to give you ideas, tips and training to help you to sell lots of product. You get orders through catalogs, online, home or office parties, events like holiday gift shows and such. Get customers' contact info for follow up and repeat sales.

Do not discount the value of manual labor.

GETTING A JOB

Many rural areas have seasonal employment opportunities. Check into the job possibilities before you commit to an area.

Look on the internet. Google your job description and related keywords along with the city and nearby towns you are looking at.

Pick up a local newspaper. Several if possible. Include surrounding towns. Pour over the classified ads as well as paid advertising. Businesses may not be hiring yet, but you can stop by and fill out an application or request an interview.

Check job boards online (monster, .gov sites,etc.) and at local markets, the post office, feed stores.

Investigate local businesses – ski areas, resorts, stone yards, construction companies, lumber yards, warehouses. Restaurants, hospitals, libraries, schools, fast food, supermarkets, etc.

Do not discount the value of manual labor. Many of these jobs are really fun for awhile. Maybe not just the job itself, but your co-workers, the customers, and the atmosphere can all add up to a pleasant experience for a few months or years.

.

Seasonal work also has its advantages. You may not get a year-round paycheck, but you do get chunks of time off. If you budget for this, it could turn into a very profitable situation. Paycheck during the season, time to build a business during the off-season. You can also be adventurous. Try something you've never thought about doing before. You may find you enjoy waiting tables, grooming ski slopes, or cleaning yards for part of the year.

Keep your present job and telecommute.

REMOTE WORKING

Keep your present job and telecommute. Many employers are trying to keep overhead down by getting employees to work fewer hours or work one or more days from home. If most of your work involves word processing, data bases, or phone-based customer service, this may be an option for you.

Does your present employer offer the opportunity to telecommute?

It doesn't hurt to ask. Are there any other employees who are working remotely? Find out if your position qualifies. Or just ask the boss.

Is your job a good fit for telecommuting?
Even if you occasionally have to meet with clients in person, if the bulk of your work is computer and phone based it has potential for remote working.

Work up a plan and present it to your boss. See if they might be open to the idea. Throw out a few feelers first, see how they respond.

Caution – do not do this until you have something else lined up if there is a risk that you will lose your job over it.

If you have unlimited funds, fine, but most of us turn to the homestead not only to escape the rat race but also to save money.

MAKING A LIVING FROM THE HOMESTEAD ITSELF

Frugal living – cut back living expenses and lifestyle to fit your smaller budget.

If you have unlimited funds, fine, but most of us turn to the homestead not only to escape the rat race but also to save money. I cover many homesteading and frugal living practices in Book 2: Milking the Wild Goat or How to Set up your Homestead. Here are some ideas to help you actually to make a business out of your homestead.

Put in some RV hookups and rent out a space or two on a nightly basis.

Put in a porta-potty and a picnic table and rent tent spaces.

Rent space for signage if your property is along highway.

Rent space for solar panels or wind turbines to the power company.

Bed and breakfast – rent out an extra room or two and provide coffee, tea, and breads, muffins, fruit or some other choices for breakfast. Check regulations in your area. See what other bed and breakfasts are providing and charging.

AirBnB – rent out a room or your whole house on a nightly or short term basis. Most areas do not yet regulate this, but some are beginning to, as complaints from neighbors arise, and homeowners (gasp) start making a little extra money from it.

Hostel – put bunks and locking storage cubes in a couple of rooms, dedicate one bathroom (with a shower) for guest use, and set up your kitchen to share with guests.

If you have the acreage, you might be able to board horses, dogs, or other pets.

Always check restrictions, licensing requirements and reporting requirements in each area before you start marketing your business. You do not want to find out later that you need a license or certification to perform some service. The fines could put you out of business and make life very unpleasant instead of wonderful.

Also, check with your insurance company about liability coverage, business coverage, or any other insurance that might be wise to ensure the continuing operation of your business in case of damage claims.

Dairy – if you are planning to get dairy animals, chances are you are going to have a lot of extra milk. You are also likely to run into people who will practically beg you to buy your extra milk. This is a nice problem to have. Nevertheless, make sure you know your local regulations. There will also be people determined to turn you in for selling raw milk. The possibilities for selling raw milk vary from state to state. Some states require a cow share agreement between dairyman and customer; some states allow the sale of state certified raw milk in farmers market type stores; some states will allow sales "for pet use only, not for human consumption". Who'da thunk there was a black market for milk?

Farmers Market – if you are on a main road, you could set up a little produce stand to sell your extra garden vegetables and such. If not, look for a local farmer's market, or start one, to sell your excess produce.

Hay – if grass grows like crazy on your property,

think about selling what you do not need for your own animals. Learn what kinds of grasses to grow for feed, how to keep out weeds, how to cut and bale hay.

Christmas tree farm – this is a good seasonal business. Make sure your land is viable for growing fir, pine, spruce, and other varieties of Christmas trees. Take water into consideration, as well. Find out how long it takes from seedling to marketable product and start building a clientele for your trees. Or set up your own tree lots.

Egg Sales – Make sure this will pay off for you. Remember you still have to feed the chickens and keep them healthy, housed, and safe. Most people will pay more for farm fresh eggs, especially if they know you are treating the chickens well.

Cattle, pig, or other meat ranch – local regulations vary on this. Check your zoning, also. If you have the acreage and facilities, you could raise a few head of cattle, pigs, goats, sheep, chickens, turkeys or other meat animals. Depending on local laws, you could set this up as a cooperative, taking payments from co-owners at various stages of the animals' life, and arranging for slaughter and butchering with a locally licensed butcher shop.

Fish farm – tilapia, etc.; Make your backyard pond

pay off. Be aware that the more fish you raise, the bigger the issues with waste disposal and pond health. Check with local restaurants to see if they buy from private parties. Find out what the local guidelines are for selling fresh fish.

Petting zoo – allow visitors to feed and interact with your critters in an enclosed, safe environment, for a fee. Sell handfuls of feed to help encourage the animals to be friendly.

Dude ranch – a bed and breakfast, with the added liability factor of horseback riding and other activities. On the other hand, part of the "experience" could include helping with ranch chores, such as feeding, mucking, watering, and such.

Homemade jams, pickles, breads, etc. – some states now have "cottage industries" regulations, which enable mom-and-pops to sell limited quantities of homemade foods, properly labeled according to their regulations, without having to install or use a separate commercial kitchen. This is a boon to home canners, bakers, and candy makers, who just want to sell a few of their extra jams, pickles, breads, and such at the farmer's market or other event. Check your local regulations; this could be a lucrative option.

Sell wool from your sheep, llamas, or other wool

producing animal. You can sell it raw (unprocessed) to private parties and commercial businesses; washed and carded (yarn shops); spun; or even as a finished item – felted, woven, knitted, or crocheted.

What natural products does your land produce? Rock, cinders, trees (sustainable firewood/lumber), sand. Contractors and homeowners are always looking for various kinds of building materials and there is not always a conveniently located home improvement store.

CONCLUSION

T he great homesteading adventure continues. The place is a work in progress. At this time we are embarking on another adventure which will put us homesteading on the road quite a bit. But the old place is not forgotten and there are still plans to continue with improvements for sustainable living and a more permanent return some day. Right now I'm trying to figure out how to travel in a ten foot trailer with two adults, an active boy, a pit bull, two laying hens and a milk goat...

RESOURCES FOR MORE INFO

WEBSITES:

note – if link does not work, try to copy and paste into your address bar.

Mrs. D's Homestead – my website and blog, where I write about our adventures from moving out of the city, to setting up and running our homestead, to transitioning to full-time rving/roadsteading. http://www.mrsdshomestead.com.

Homesteading With Mrs. D – my Grit Magazine reader blog. Here I post other items of interest about homesteading. http://www.grit.com/blogs/homesteading-with-mrs-d.aspx

Pure Living for Life – one couple's journey off grid to become debt-free, more sustainable, and location independent.

http://purelivingforlife.com/6-ways-we-make-money-online-while-homesteading/

Homesteading – one of a conglomerate of sites dedicated to different topics. Covers a wide variety of homesteading topics by different authors.

https://homesteading.com/ways-make-money-homesteading/

Legal Zoom - free small biz startup kit with 3 ebooks and 25 discounts.
Legal forms and services.

https://www.legalzoom.com/

Entrepreneur - 50 tips for starting your own company. Also a good website for business tips.

https://www.entrepreneur.com/article/235903

Small Business Administration - lots of free info from the government in regards to starting and running your business.

https://www.sba.gov/starting-business/how-start-business/10-steps-starting-business

BOOKS:

All books are available on Amazon as of the date of this writing.

$100 startup by Chris Guillebeau - shows you how to lead of life of adventure, meaning and purpose – and earn a good living.

Still in his early thirties, Chris is on the verge of completing a tour of every country on earth – he has already visited more than 175 nations – and yet he has never held a "real job" or earned a regular paycheck. Rather, he has a special genius for turning ideas into income, and he uses what he earns both to support his life of adventure and to give back.

https://www.amazon.com/100-Startup-Reinvent-Living-Create-ebook/dp/B0067TGSOK/ref=sr_1_4?s=books&ie=UTF8&qid=1488915151&sr=1-4&keywords=how+to+start+your+own+business

Start your own business – by the Inc staff at Entrepreneur Media

Tapping into more than 33 years of small business expertise, the staff at Entrepreneur Media takes today's entrepreneurs beyond opening their doors and through the first three years of ownership. This revised edition features amended chapters on choosing a business, adding partners, getting funded, and managing the business structure and employees, and includes help understanding the latest tax and healthcare reform information and legalities.

https://www.amazon.com/Start-Your-Own-Business-Sixth-ebook/dp/B00R3L71WE/ref=sr_1_1?s=books&ie=UTF8&qid=1488916304&sr=1-1&keywords=how+to+start+a+business

Leave the grind behind by Justin Gesso

Get the bestselling book that shows you how to make more money, build your legacy, and quit your job. This book is dedicated to all those ready to forge their own path, get more out of life, and burn their imprint on the world. You want more money, more freedom, and to build your own legacy. Perhaps you want to carve a future by leveraging your talents to freelance, consult, or become an entrepreneur. https://www.amazon.com/dp/B01J4AGOQU?psc=1

YOU TUBE CHANNELS OF INTEREST

Mrs. D's Homestead – my You Tube Channel where I post videos about homesteading, homeschooling, simple living; full-time rving; handmade soaps, lotions and folk crafts.

https://www.youtube.com/user/mrsdshomestead/videos

How to start a business in 10 days by Entrepreneur

https://www.youtube.com/watch?v=gLOgTyMtk6c

How to turn your homesteading hobby into a business by Homesteady

https://www.youtube.com/watch?v=giMkErPwMB4

Make your homestead profitable by DirtPatch-Heaven

https://www.youtube.com/watch?v=gEOBTMevXqo

CAN YOU HELP ME, PLEASE?

I hope you have enjoyed Escape the City and Thrive - Book 3: Paying for the Dream – or - How to Thrive on Your Homestead, as much as I enjoyed writing it.

I would be so grateful if you would leave a review on my website at:

http://mrsdshomestead.com/site/shop/books-n-downloads/escape-the-city-and-thrive/

In return, if you will leave me your email address on any of my webpages in the newsletter sign up box, I will keep you updated about new book releases, free downloads, quick tips for homesteading, homeschooling and simple living and my latest blog posts, all in one weekly-or-so newsletter!

ABOUT THE AUTHOR

Robyn Dolan escaped the city for the first time in 1986, as a young mother, with her second child on the way. The family moved to Big Bear Lake, CA and she lived and sold Real Estate there among the tall pines, deep lake and hordes of skiers for 12 years.

After her divorce, Ms. Dolan decided to move even farther out and eventually settled in Ash Fork, Arizona, "50 miles from everywhere", west of Flagstaff and north of Prescott. Here she raised goats, sheep, chickens, horses, dogs, cats, the occasional pig, and a milk cow, for another 14 years. She also gave birth to her fourth child in Arizona.

Presently, the author is living full time in her 26 foot travel trailer, traveling between elderly grandpas and enjoying the sights in between. She calls her continuing attempts at homesteading and frugal living "roadsteading" and her son's homeschooling experience "roadschooling".